REPENTANCE

Repentance
A Guide to Receiving God's Forgiveness

Michael Scanlan, T.O.R.

SERVANT BOOKS
Ann Arbor, Michigan

Published by Servant Books
P.O. Box 8617
Ann Arbor, Michigan 48107

Cover design by Charles Piccirilli and Robert Coe
Cover photo by Four By Five, Inc.

90 91 92 93 10 9 8 7 6 5 4 3 2

Printed in the United States of America
ISBN 0-89283-398-X

Contents

Acknowledgment

The authors of the *Catholic Bible Study Guides* wish to acknowledge the invaluable contribution made by Nick Cavnar in developing the format for individual study used in these guides.

Introduction

"Repent!"

None of us likes to hear that word very much. It conjures up visions of punishment, humiliation, and guilt. But that was the message that Jesus preached when he walked the earth. It is the message that he sent his apostles to preach. It is the message that the church has proclaimed from the very beginning. In fact, it should not be a frightening message at all, but one that brings forgiveness, peace, joy, and healing into our lives.

Repentance is really nothing other than the way to a close and intimate relationship with God. Rather than bringing punishment, it is the way to avoid eternal punishment by sharing in Christ's word of redemption on the cross. If it brings momentary humiliation, it brings eternal exaltation, as Jesus said, "Whoever humbles himself will be exalted" (Mt 23:12). And far from pressing guilt upon us, repentance is the only way to be relieved of the guilt that comes from sin.

What on earth could be better than that?

This guide presents important truths and understandings about repentance from Scripture, with a special focus on how repentance can become a part of our daily life. I will be sharing with you in particular what God has taught me about repentance in my own life. God has brought me to repentance on many occasions, and I have experienced the fruit of this important scriptural teaching time and again. I can testify personally that the fruit of the repentance-filled life is indeed the forgiveness, the peace, the joy, and the healing only God can bring. But the important part of this guide is neither my experience nor my advice; it is the Word of God in Scripture that has power to transform your understanding of this essential of the Christian life.

How to Use this Guide

There are many ways to study Scripture. Scholars gain expertise in the original biblical languages and other ancient tongues that are contemporaneous with the development and writing of the Scriptures. They become experts in biblical history, archeology, and linguistics, all in an effort to help us understand the meaning of the inspired authors. Their work can contribute to our understanding. In fact, if you have a popular commentary, it probably includes some of the insights and knowledge Scripture scholars have gleaned in their studies. But this is not the focus of our particular study. You do not need to be a biblical linguist, nor do you need the specialized training of an archeologist or a historian. This study simply approaches the Bible as the Word of God and seeks to discover the basic meaning of the text so we can apply it to our lives today.

All you really need to use this guide profitably is a Bible and a heart and a mind open to what God has to say about repentance. The guide provides space to write down answers to the study questions and to fill out the charts and exercises in each individual study. You might also find it helpful to write down your thoughts and reflections in a notebook. Of course, make wise use of any other study helps you already know how to use. These might include a commentary, a Bible dictionary, or a concordance.

Each of the nine studies should take at least an hour. Set aside a little more than an hour for each study and try to work without interruptions. Always begin your study with prayer. Ask God to help you understand his Word, then proceed in a spirit of heartfelt prayer. So the truth of God's Word can sink in, pause occasionally to reflect on what he is teaching you.

The nine individual, hour-long studies in this guide are divided into three parts that build steadily in your understanding of repentance. The first part explores what repentance is, why it is an essential part of the gospel message, how some basic attitudes of the mind and heart can block repentance, and then how genuine repentance enables us to receive God's forgiveness and love. The second part is devoted entirely to identifying common pitfalls that hinder us from repenting— despairing of God's mercy, failing to realize how unlimited that mercy really is, and entertaining occasions of sin by living in a twilight zone between sin and virtue. The third part of the guide shows us the importance of living a life of ongoing conversion and repentance, so God can not only deal with patterns of sin but also release his healing into our lives. God gives us the grace for this life of ongoing conversion in the seven sacraments. The Eucharist is the primary sacrament of healing and strengthening. The two sacraments that especially focus on repentance and forgiveness are the sacrament of reconciliation (penance) and, in times of sickness, the sacrament of the anointing of the sick.

You'll find that each individual study will explore some facet of repentance by focusing on one or more key Scripture passages. To help direct your time, I have opened each study with a brief commentary.

Keep in mind, though, that the heart of the studies consists of questions and exercises where you investigate the Scriptures in depth with a focus on some aspect of repentance. It is important that you look up every Scripture referred to and follow my instructions carefully. That way you will get the most out of your study. It will also help you realize that God's Word is a unity, and each part helps us understand the whole when studied in context.

Each of the nine lessons also contains a tip for repenting of sin and receiving God's forgiveness. This is a way of applying the message of the commentary and your study of Scripture to everyday life. Read these tips over carefully and try to use them. In fact, you might find it helpful to put one into practice each week as you go through the guide. They will help make receiving God's forgiveness more of a reality in your life.

At the end of each study, there is an optional memory verse. If you memorize this verse, you will have in your mind a brief summary of the study you've just completed. Christians have found that memorizing and "chewing on" God's Word has helped them to live it out by the Word of God since the earliest days of the church.

Of course, the most important aid to this study is the Holy Spirit. He is the one who inspired the writing of the Scriptures in the first place. He is the one who changes our hearts so we can turn back to God and receive forgiveness for our sins. Ask for his help as you make your way through this guide.

Questions for Group Discussion

You'll notice that I have included five questions for group discussion at the end of each individual study. I do recommend that you go through the study guide with a group from your local parish, prayer group, or community—if that's possible. We are meant to listen and reflect on God's Word as his people and not simply as individuals. You will benefit from the insight and practical help offered by your brothers and sisters in Christ.

Group members will need to commit themselves to finishing each study before meeting as a group. Also you'll want to develop a format, an approach to leadership, and a set time for your group meetings. I strongly suggest that you open and close each group discussion with a short time of prayer. It might be helpful as well to have someone read the main Scripture passage for study before you begin your discussion. That way the passage for study will be fresh in everyone's mind. After the formal close of your group meetings, consider taking some time for informal fellowship. This will give group members a chance to get to know each other better in a more relaxed atmosphere.

As you set up your time and format for group meetings, keep in mind that the questions for discussion should be used flexibly, depending on the needs of your group. If you spend a full discussion session on one question, that's all right. Depending on the nature of your group, you may even want to develop some of your own questions for discussion.

My sincere prayer is that as you use this guide, you will come to a deeper understanding of the call to repentance, so you can receive God's forgiveness and experience more of his abundant mercy and steadfast love.

Part I:

Responding to the Call to Repent

We first need to understand what repentance is and why it is an essential part of the gospel message. Then we can turn to some basic attitudes of the mind and heart that block repentance and show how repentance enables us to receive God's forgiveness and love. Our first three studies will lay a foundation by covering these critical areas. Once these basics are understood, we can turn to Parts II and III which discuss some common pitfalls or misunderstandings about repentance and explain how we are called to a life of ongoing conversion to Christ—including regular reception of the sacraments and the release of healing in our lives.

Study 1—Matthew 3:1-12
The Call to Repentance

In those days John the Baptist appeared, preaching in the desert of Judea and saying, "Repent, for the kingdom of heaven is at hand!" It was of him that the prophet Isaiah had spoken when he said,
"A voice of one crying out in the desert,
'Prepare the way of the Lord,
make straight his paths.'"
John wore clothing made of camel's hair and had a leather belt around his waist. His food was locusts and wild honey. At that time Jerusalem, all Judea, and the whole region around the Jordan were going out to him and were being baptized by him in the Jordan River as they acknowledged their sins. (Mt 3:1-6)

In each of the Gospels, the story of Jesus' ministry begins in the same way, with John the Baptist's call to repentance. John "appeared," says Matthew. Mark says the same (Mk 1:4). Luke tells us that at a certain time "the word of God came to John" (Lk 3:2), and that word was a message of repentance. The apostle John begins his Gospel with a description of John the Baptist and his ministry (Jn 1:6-28), focusing on his testimony to Jesus. And when Jesus begins his ministry on earth, how does he begin? With the same message: "Repent, for the kingdom of heaven is at hand" (Mt 4:17).

The admonition to repent is one of the most frequently repeated in Scripture. The great prophets of the Old Testament based their message on the call to repent. Isaiah, Jeremiah, Ezekiel, Amos, Hosea, Joel—all these prophets preached a message of repentance. Joel urges the people to "rend your hearts" in sorrow for "your" sins and to return to the Lord. Isaiah gives the Lord's promise that he will restore a repentant people: "For a brief moment I abandoned you, but with great tenderness I will take you back" (Is 54:7).

Not only did Jesus proclaim a message of repentance, he also commissioned his disciples to do likewise (Mk 6:12). After the resurrection, when the young church began to proclaim the gospel, the message was still the same. When the crowds asked Peter how they should respond to his preaching, he said, "Repent and be baptized, every one of you" (Acts 2:38). Proclaiming the gospel to the Gentiles at

Athens, Paul told them, "God has overlooked the times of ignorance, but now he demands that all people everywhere repent" (Acts 17:30).

The Lord's call to repentance is not just for those outside the church. In the Book of Revelation, the Lord gives John messages for seven churches. Of these, five are messages of repentance, wholly or in part. The Lord calls Christians to be eager to repent: "Those whom I love, I reprove and chastise. Be earnest, therefore, and repent" (Rv 3:19).

No matter how many times we have committed our life to the Lord, then, we need to be eager to hear the message of repentance. We can understand this need better by grasping the nature of repentance. The word for repentance in the New Testament is *metanoia,* literally a "turning of the mind." The underlying concept of repentance is a turning or change of direction. In a Christian context, this means turning from sin or what is not of God to virtue or what is of God. Even when we have turned from sin before, if our lives are not headed directly for God, we can still use more turning.

At one point in my life, I served as a deckhand in the U.S. Merchant Marine. Most of the time, my assignment was to man the wheel and maintain the course we were following from Honolulu to the Panama Canal. I was under the command of the mate, and from time to time he would call me and tell me to change course. He was not changing his mind about what direction we should follow. Rather, he had discovered that we were not, in fact, going in exactly the right direction. So we needed to turn the ship one way or another in order to proceed directly to our destination. You could say that we were "repenting" of our former course every time I made a change of direction.

In the same way, we need to be eager for God to show us our sin so that we can repent. We should not consider the discovery of sin and turning from sin as an occasion of sadness. It is an opportunity for God to work, to keep us on a straight course toward him.

Study: Matthew 3:1-12.

1. Read verses 1-3.
The prophecy that is applied to John the Baptist here is a quotation from the book of Isaiah, chapter 40. Read Isaiah 40:1-11. What is the message being presented here?

_____

_____

_____

How is John the Baptist fulfilling Isaiah's message? Be specific. What does this tell us about John the Baptist's role in preparing "the way of the Lord?"

a) _____

_____

_____

b) _____

_____

John's message was one of repentance. How does the prophecy in Isaiah deal with repentance? How does it deal with the results of repentance?

a) _____

_____

_____

b) _____

_____

John the Baptist's message of repentance was to "prepare the way of the Lord." How can I make a "highway" for God in my life?

_____

_____

_____

_____

_____

_____

2. Read verses 4-6.

These verses speak of the people who came to John to repent. They are referred to at greater length in the account in Luke 3:10-14. Read this passage. John gives three kinds of directions to different sorts of people. The first appears to be directed to all those who came to him. What is it?

_____

How can I apply this message in my own life? Think of at least two ways you can apply this message.

a) _____

_____

_____

b) _____

_____

The next two directions deal with two groups whose occupations made them generally hated, and with good reason. Tax collectors were the agents of the Roman occupiers. The soldiers referred to were probably Roman soldiers, who also represented the foreign occupation. What does John tell them to do?

_____

_____

How can I apply what John told them to my life? Think of two personal areas where you can apply this direction.

a) _____

_____

_____

b) _____

_____

3. Read verses 7-12.

In these verses Matthew describes how John addressed the Pharisees and Sadducees, both groups who had reason to believe that they were knowledgeable about religion and personally righteous. John then speaks of Jesus, who is to come after him, baptizing in the Holy Spirit and in fire.

What does John say to the Pharisees and Sadducees? Sum it up in your own words.

_____

_____

Look at some of the places where Jesus addresses the Pharisees especially: Matthew 23 and Luke 11:37-54. Based on what Jesus says here, what things about the Pharisees would warrant John's harsh words? List your points below. Number them for future reference.

_____

_____

_____

_____

_____

_____

_____

_____

Why should a reference to the coming of Jesus accompany these words to the Pharisees? (Compare Lk 7:24-30)

_____

_____

_____

_____

_____

How have I been like a Pharisee in my own life? Take a moment for reflection and be honest with yourself.

_____

_____

_____

_____

_____

What are two attitudes that can help or hinder my own coming to Jesus?

a) _____

_____

b) _____

_____

Summary:

Look over your notes from this study. What have you learned about the nature of repentance, the necessity for repentance, and the results of repentance?

1. The nature of repentance: _____

_____

2. The necessity for repentance: _____

_____

3. The results of repentance: _____

Tip for Repentance:

Perhaps the biggest obstacle we face when we first hear the call to repentance is fear. The very word can strike terror into our hearts. We are afraid of punishment, of condemnation, and of the prospect of having to change in ways that are very hard to take. In this connection it can be helpful to remember the word for repentance in the New Testament, which I have mentioned in my commentary: *metanoia*. The original meaning of the word is a change of mind or an attitude of the heart toward something. Repentance, then, is something that happens first of all in our minds and hearts. Fears about repentance often originate in certain attitudes of the mind and heart that make us reluctant to change. If you feel you are having difficulty with the idea of repentance, try asking God to change your mind and your heart about sin, to give you a new attitude toward sin and toward your life. That change of mind and heart is in itself a starting point and an essential part of repentance.

Optional Memory Verse:

"Those whom I love, I reprove and chastise. Be earnest, therefore, and repent." (Rv 3:19)

For Group Discussion:

1. Why is John the Baptist's role important in preparing "the way of the Lord?" Explain.

2. Why do you think the message of repentance is mentioned so often throughout the Bible?

3. Is the message of repentance meant only for those who are outside the church? Discuss.

4. What exactly is the meaning of the word "repentance" in the New Testament?

5. Why were both John the Baptist and Jesus particularly harsh at times in their dealings with the Pharisees and Sadducees? What does this tell us about the importance of our attitude of heart in responding to the call to repentance? Discuss.

Study 2—Luke 8:4-15
Responding to the Word

"A sower went out to sow his seed. And as he sowed, some seed fell on the path and was trampled, and the birds of the sky ate it up. Some seed fell on rocky ground, and when it grew, it withered for lack of moisture. Some seed fell among thorns, and the thorns grew with it and choked it. And some seed fell on good soil, and when it grew, it produced fruit a hundredfold." (Lk 8:5-8)

Repentance doesn't happen spontaneously, and it doesn't happen automatically. We repent in response to God's action, to his call to repent found in his Word, in his law, and in our consciences. And we need to respond to this call—God can't do it for us. The parable of the sower tells us about the different ways that people can respond to the word of repentance.

Jesus explained the meaning of this parable to his disciples after he had told it publicly. "The seed is the word of God," he told them. "Those on the path are the ones who have heard, but the devil comes and takes away the word from their hearts that they may not believe and be saved" (Lk 8:11-12). This is the first way people can react. These are the people who don't give God's Word a chance, so that it's like seed that someone stomps on or the birds eat up. They allow the first distraction to blind their eyes and stop their ears. Jesus says that they are allowing the devil himself to rob them of their chance to believe and be saved.

The second situation, the seed that falls on rocky ground, "are the ones who, when they hear, receive the word with joy, but they have no root; they believe only for a time and fall away in time of trial" (Lk 8:13). The rocky ground is the hard heart of people who are just not interested in changing any more. There might be some soil in rocky ground, but not very much. The Word of God can't go very far. These people may believe it and receive it into their hearts, but they don't do anything with it. They say, "Isn't that nice." Then such people let the Word of God simply sit there until other concerns take over. Thus they forget the Word that God has spoken.

"As for the seed that fell among thorns," Jesus says, "they are the ones who have heard, but as they go along, they are choked by the anxieties and riches and pleasures of life, and they fail to produce mature fruit"

(Lk 8:14). The thorns are bondage, things that hold us captive: attachment to sin, to the world's ways of thinking, to anxiety and worry about our life, to self-centeredness, to things and people we don't want to get out of our lives even though we know that God wants them out. In this case, when we take the Word into our lives and don't do anything about the thorns, the thorns choke the Word right out.

In the final case, the seed falls on good soil. Jesus explains that "they are the ones who, when they have heard the word, embrace it with a generous and good heart, and bear fruit through perseverance" (Lk 8:15). And look what happens to this seed: it yields a harvest, an abundant harvest of a hundredfold. That's what we want to happen in our lives when we hear the Word of God—we want it to bring forth a fruitful harvest for the glory of God our Father and for the advancement of his eternal kingdom.

God's Word tells us to produce fruit for God. That is what John the Baptist told those Pharisees who came to him for baptism, the ones who thought that they were already virtuous. He told them, "Produce good fruit as evidence of your repentance" (Mt 3:8). We cannot expect to produce good fruit simply by believing the Word but refusing to change. We have to repent of everything in our lives that is incompatible with a godly life. We need to decide to change these things. It is not enough merely to feel sorry; the key is actually to change our lives in the area in question. Then God's Word can bear fruit in us.

Study: Luke 8:4-15.

1. Read verses 4-5 and 9-12. Here Jesus presents the first response: those whose hearts are hard, so that the Word does not penetrate. How have I responded this way in my life? Once again, be specific and be honest with yourself. Number your points.

_____

_____

_____

_____

Read 2 Samuel 12:1-25, the story of David's repentance. How did David allow the Word of God to penetrate his heart? What was its effect?

a) _____

_____

_____

_____

b) _____

_____

_____

_____

How can I respond more like David to God's word of repentance in my life? Number your points below.

_____

_____

_____

_____

_____

2. Read verses 6 and 13. The second response is that of the rocky ground, where the Word springs up but has no depth. How has this response been a part of my life? Reread the commentary if necessary and number your points.

_____

_____

_____

_____

_____

Read 2 Kings 22:1-23:30, the story of King Josiah of Judah. How does Josiah respond to the Word of the Lord? How does he show that it had taken root in him?

a) _____

_____

_____

_____

b) _____

_____

_____

_____

How can I respond more like Josiah to God's Word in my life? Mention one major area and be specific.

_____

_____

_____

_____

_____

3. Read verses 7 and 14.
Here Jesus contrasts those who allow distractions and anxieties to choke the Word with those who bear good fruit. How have I allowed the cares and distractions of the world to choke out God's Word in my life? Try to pinpoint at least two areas.

a) _____

_____

b) _____

Read Acts 22:2-21 and 2 Corinthians 11:22-29 where Paul talks about his conversion and subsequent career. What obstacles did Paul face in carrying out his repentance? How did his perseverance bear fruit?

a) _____

b) _____

How can I imitate Paul in overcoming distractions and bearing fruit for the Lord? Is there one distraction that has been particularly troublesome for me? Describe it below.

a) _____

b) _____

4. Read verses 8 and 15.

Here Jesus speaks of those who bear good fruit. In Galatians 5:13-26, Paul speaks of the differing fruits of the flesh and the spirit. What kinds of things are the deeds of the flesh?

_____

_____

_____

What are the fruit of the spirit?

_____

_____

_____

The works of the flesh are some of the thorns that can spring up and choke out the Word of God. Give three examples of these works.

a) _____

b) _____

c) _____

How am I rooting out the "thorns" in my life and cultivating the fruit of the spirit? Don't forget to number your points.

_____

_____

_____

_____

_____

_____

_____

_____

Summary:

Read over your notes from this study. How can you better respond to the word of repentance in your life? Write out a simple and manageable plan for responding to the word of repentance in one key area of your personal life. Remember to be both realistic and honest.

1. My objective: _____

_____

_____

2. My schedule for accomplishing it: _____

_____

_____

3. My deadline for accomplishing it: _____

_____

_____

Tip for Repentance:

We can't begin to respond to God's Word until we hear it. One of the benefits of regular reading of the Scriptures is that through it God will often show us how we need to repent. While God has many ways in which he can speak to us, his inspired Word in Scripture is especially reliable and effective. If you are not regularly reading the Bible, start today.

If you are already reading the Bible regularly, you have probably experienced God speaking to you through it. If you haven't, or just wish that you could hear him more, try these approaches. When you read the Bible, consciously think, "How does my life compare with what is written here? How can I apply this commandment to my life?"

Another way to allow God's Word to call us on is to read over those places where God's standards are presented, reviewing our life in comparison to them. Some of the key passages are:

Exodus 20:1-17—The Ten Commandments
Matthew, chapters 5, 6, and 7—The Sermon on the Mount
Matthew 22:34-40—The great commandments
Galatians 5:16-26—The flesh and the spirit
Ephesians 4:25-6:9—Standards for Christian living

Consider taking a couple of weeks to review these Scripture passages. Set aside a short period of time for reading, reflection, and prayer every day. Be faithful to it, and let God's Word speak to you.

Optional Memory Verse:

Therefore, put away all filth and evil excess and humbly welcome the word that has been planted in you and is able to save your souls.

(Jas 1:21)

For Group Discussion:

1. Hardness of heart can block God's Word from getting into our lives. How does this happen?

2. Attachments to the things of this world can choke out God's Word in our lives. Many Christians think Americans are particularly prone to this danger. Do you agree? Discuss.

3. Jesus tells us that if we are open to God's Word and respond to it with "a generous and good heart," we will bear much fruit for the kingdom of God. Why is repentance key to responding to God's Word and bearing fruit for the kingdom of God?

4. Discuss the examples of David and Josiah as men who responded to God's Word and repented.

5. Why is reading and reflecting on Scripture regularly a helpful way to respond to God's Word about repentance?

Study 3—Luke 7:36-50
Forgiveness and Love

Then [Jesus] turned to the woman and said to Simon, "Do you see this woman? When I entered your house, you did not give me water for my feet, but she has bathed them with her tears and wiped them with her hair. You did not give me a kiss, but she has not ceased kissing my feet since the time I entered. You did not anoint my head with oil, but she anointed my feet with ointment. So I tell you, her many sins have been forgiven; hence, she has shown great love. But the one to whom little is forgiven, loves little." He said to her, "Your sins are forgiven." The others at table said to themselves, "Who is this who even forgives sins?" But he said to the woman, "Your faith has saved you; go in peace." (Lk 7:44-50)

This was not a woman who had sinned just once. This was not a woman who had sinned in secret. She had sinned so many times that her whole identity in the town was as "a sinful woman" (Lk 7:37). Traditionally, we identify her with Mary Magdalene, who became a follower of Jesus. What was her sin? Many have thought that she was a prostitute—certainly a public and notorious way of sinning, one particularly odious to so-called decent people. The Pharisee who had invited Jesus to dinner knew her. As he watched her fall at Jesus' feet, washing them with her tears and drying them with her hair, kissing them and anointing them with precious ointment, he wondered how a prophet could not know what kind of woman she was. No rabbi would want to be touched by such a woman, so filled with impurity and uncleanness.

Jesus knew her. He knew her better than Simon the Pharisee did. The words he spoke to her assured her of forgiveness. More than that, they assure us as well that repentance is not something that ends in pain and misery. It is an occasion of joy and love. In the end Jesus says, "Your faith has saved you; go in peace."

Jesus illustrates the fruit of repentance by telling Simon a short parable. "'Two people were in debt to a certain creditor; one owed five hundred days' wages and the other owed fifty. Since they were unable to repay the debt, he forgave it for both. Which of them will love him more?' Simon said in reply, 'The one, I suppose, whose larger debt was forgiven'" (Lk 7:41-43). More forgiveness means more love. The love that Simon had shown to Jesus was very small, but Mary Magdalene's was very great. Therefore, Simon should see not that she was a greater sinner than he was but that she has been forgiven more.

In fact, Mary's great love was an indication that she had truly repented of her sins from the heart. It is one of the fruits of genuine repentance, for Christian love is not possible unless someone has really repented of sin.

Thus Mary Magdalene came to Jesus with tears of genuine repentance, sorrowing for her sins but believing that Jesus could forgive them. And so she has been throughout Christian history a great model of repentance. Scripture records that she had had seven demons cast out of her (Lk 8:2). Her forgiveness was accompanied by being freed from the demonic influences that had come over her through her life of sin. But note that forgiveness came first.

The example of Mary Magdalene should give us great cause for hope. Even if we feel that there are things in our life that we can't control, we can still repent of the sins they cause. Even if we say, "I've confessed this lying or cheating or resentment or this pattern of losing my temper or sexual impurity before—I promised that I would never to do it again, and now I've failed again," we still should never let that stop us from going to the Lord for forgiveness.

Later, it was the same Mary Magdalene who stood by Jesus at the foot of the cross and who was one of the first witnesses to the resurrection. The result of her repentance was the tremendous privilege of loving and following Jesus. Jesus came for sinners, and we can trust in his forgiveness whenever we turn to him from our hearts. We should remember and meditate on the words of Jesus, "Your faith has saved you; go in peace." Our joy can be very great in being forgiven sinners.

Study: Luke 7:36-50.

1. Read verses 26-39.
What does Mary Magdalene do to indicate her repentance?

_____

_____

Which are signs of her love for Jesus?

_____

_____

What does her action show about her belief in Jesus?

_____

_____

What does the Pharisee's response show about his attitude toward sin and sinners?

_____

_____

What does the Pharisee's response show about his belief regarding Jesus?

_____

_____

How can Mary Magdalene inspire you in your daily life to repent and accept God's forgiveness for your sin? Is there some area of your life where you feel particularly stirred in your heart by her example? Describe the area in question. Then tell how Mary Magdalene's example can help you respond in the right way.

a) _____

_____

_____

b) _____

_____

_____

2. Read verses 40-43.
Jesus uses debt as a metaphor for sin in other parables. One of these is found in Matthew 18:21-35. Read that passage and compare it to this

one. What is Jesus saying our attitude toward God should be?

_____

_____

_____

_____

What should our attitude toward other people be?

_____

_____

_____

How is Jesus correcting the Pharisee here? What attitude of heart is Jesus seeking?

a) _____

_____

_____

b) _____

_____

_____

How does my life compare with the standard Jesus is presenting in these parables? Remember to be specific and number your points.

_____

_____

_____

_____

_____

_____

_____

3. Read verses 44-50.
Here Jesus praises the sinful woman's response, which indicates genuine repentance, and forgives her sins. Compare this encounter with some similar instances in the Gospels. In each case, how does Jesus deal with the sinner? How does the sinner respond? What can you learn from the sinner's response? Fill out the chart that has been provided.

The Scripture Passage and the Human Party Involved	How Jesus Deals with the Sinner	How the Sinner Responds	What I Can Learn from the Sinner's Response
The Samaritan woman (Jn 4:4-30)			
The woman taken in adultery (Jn 8:4-11)			
Zacchaeus (Lk 19:1-10)			

Summary:

Look over your notes from this study. What can you see about how Jesus treats sinners? How can you apply this to your own life?

1. How Jesus treats sinners: _____

_____

_____

_____

2. How I can apply this teaching: _____

_____

_____

_____

Tip for Repentance:

Having the right attitude and response to God can turn repentance from a burden into a source of joy. When we understand how much we have been forgiven through the sacrifice of Jesus Christ on the cross, we are moved to gratitude and love. The pain of repentance lasts only for a moment, but the fruits of it in our lives should be permanent. We best show our love for God by coming to him regularly in prayer. In order to make repentance joyful for us as often as we do it, our prayer should regularly include thanksgiving for the forgiveness we have received.

It is also important to remember that when our sins are forgiven, we no longer need to feel guilt for them. In fact, faith in God's mercy means that we should not feel guilt. Instead, we should remember our past sins only in order to give thanks for God's mercy. Cultivating thanksgiving will not only increase our ability to rejoice in what God has done, it will also make repentance more welcome in the future.

Optional Memory Verse:

"So I tell you, her many sins have been forgiven; hence, she has shown great love." (Lk 7:47)

For Group Discussion:

1. What is wrong with Simon the Pharisee's attitude toward Mary Magdalene?

2. In contrast to Simon's attitude, why does Jesus praise Mary Magdalene? What does this tell us about the relationship between repenting of our sin and being able to receive God's love and forgiveness?

3. Why is Mary Magdalene a model of repentance for us? Hint: Examine Mary Magdalene's life in light of the meaning of the New Testament word for "repentance." Discuss.

4. How are the Samaritan woman and Zacchaeus like Mary Magdalene in their response to Jesus?

5. Let everyone in the group share an example of how God's love and forgiveness was the fruit of repentance in someone's life.

Part II

Common Pitfalls that Hinder Us from Repenting

In our last study, we saw how genuine repentance from the heart enables us to receive God's forgiveness and love. Just so, common pitfalls in repenting and receiving God's forgiveness are despairing of his mercy and failing to realize how unlimited that mercy really is. Another common pitfall is our tendency to entertain occasions of sin by living in a twilight zone between sin and virtue. The next three studies will address these problem areas with the goal of helping us 1) to appropriate the abundant mercy of God and 2) to avoid occasions of sin.

Study 4—Luke 22:54-62
Despair of God's Mercy

After arresting [Jesus] they led him away and took him into the house of the high priest; Peter was following at a distance. They lit a fire in the middle of the courtyard and sat around it, and Peter sat down with them. When a maid saw him seated in the light, she looked intently at him and said, "This man too was with him." But he denied it saying, "Woman, I do not know him." A short while later someone else saw him and said, "You too are one of them"; but Peter answered, "My friend, I am not." About an hour later, still another insisted, "Assuredly, this man was with him, for he also is a Galilean." But Peter said, "My friend, I do not know what you are talking about." Just as he was saying this, the cock crowed, and the Lord turned and looked at Peter; and Peter remembered the word of the Lord, how he had said to him, "Before the cock crows today, you will deny me three times." He went out and began to weep bitterly. (Lk 22:54-62)

Judas was not the only disciple who betrayed the Lord. Peter—whom Jesus had made leader of the apostles, the one who first acknowledged the Lord and the one to whom Jesus had entrusted the keys of the kingdom of heaven (Mt 16:16-19)—Peter himself denied that he even knew Jesus in the hour of Jesus' greatest need! This was almost as bad as the act of handing Jesus over to the authorities. But Peter's response to his sin was very different from Judas.' This teaches us something about repentance and about why some people fail to repent.

Why would someone not wish to adjust the course of his or her life so as to be more directly following the Lord? we might wonder. One common rationalization is to doubt God's mercy. This reason comes down to, "It won't do any good. Try as I may, I won't be able to set myself on the right course." This conclusion comes from the misconception that "my sin is too big—God cannot forgive me for this one." In a way, this reflects a subtle pride. We think that we can create a problem so big even God can't fix it.

Scripture is very helpful in giving us examples that demonstrate the error of such a conclusion. One is the contrasting cases of Peter and Judas. Peter denied the Lord when confronted by various bystanders during the trial of Jesus. The Lord had predicted this denial at the Last

Supper, indeed just at the point where Peter was most loudly proclaiming his willingness to die for the Lord (Mt 26:31-35). Peter remembered this prediction and realized how he had fulfilled it. After denying the Lord three times, he went out, wept, and repented for his sin. Later he publicly recommitted his life to the Lord after the resurrection (Jn 21:15-19). At that time, Jesus predicted that Peter would indeed die for him. In the end, he did die a martyr's death, passing at last the test he failed at the time of Jesus' passion.

Judas betrayed the Lord just before Peter denied him. Jesus had predicted Judas' betrayal, just as he had predicted Peter's denial. Like Peter, Judas recognized the enormity of his sin. He went back to the Sanhedrin, who had paid him to betray Jesus. Not only did he try to give them back the money he had received, he recognized that what he had done was seriously wrong. "I have sinned in betraying innocent blood," he told them (Mt 27:4). He may have thought of the special care and love that Jesus had given him as one of the twelve. Judas may have thought that because he had repaid Jesus so badly, he couldn't be forgiven. Although he recognized that he had sinned, Scripture gives us no indication that he repented. Rather, he despaired and committed suicide by going out and hanging himself (Mt 27:5).

Although Peter was also deeply distressed by the enormity of his sin, he did not despair. He knew that God's mercy and love were greater than his sin. He trusted in the Lord, repented, received forgiveness, was restored and indeed elevated to be above his brothers. His is the attitude that we should have. If we despair of God's mercy, we compound our sin by further rejecting God. We prefer our misery to God's love. Even as sinners, we cannot outdo God. We should always trust in God's forgiving love, regardless of our sins.

Study: Luke 22:54-62.

1. Read Matthew 26:14-16, John 13:21-30, John 18:1-4, and Matthew 27:3-5. These passages describe Judas' betrayal of Jesus and subsequent despair. What actions did Judas take as part of his betrayal? List them below.

What opportunities did he have to repent? Number them below.

_____

_____

_____

_____

_____

In Matthew 27, Judas clearly regrets betraying Jesus. What does he not do that he might have done?

_____

_____

_____

How have I seen Judas' temptation operating in my own life? What do I need to do to overcome this temptation?

a) _____

_____

_____

b) _____

_____

_____

2. Read Luke 22:54-62.
In Luke 22:31-34, Jesus makes a prediction about Peter. What is Peter's response to this prediction?

_____

_____

_____

_____

Peter later denies knowing Jesus at all. How does this fulfill Jesus' prediction?

_____

_____

_____

What two things stimulate Peter to repent?

_____

_____

_____

How is Peter's response different from Judas'? What is the attitude of heart that makes the difference for Peter?

a) _____

_____

_____

b) _____

_____

_____

How have I seen Jesus touch my life in the way he called Peter to repent? Mention two specific instances.

a) _____

_____

_____

b) _____

_____

_____

3. Read John 21:15-19.
How do Jesus' questions recall Peter's betrayal? List your answers below.

_____

_____

_____

_____

_____

How does what Jesus says here fulfill the prediction in Luke 22:31-32?

_____

_____

_____

_____

_____

What kinds of fruit is Peter expected to show from his repentance?

_____

_____

_____

_____

How is Jesus calling me to serve and to suffer for him? What are two areas in my life where the call to service and suffering applies?

a) _____

_____

_____

_____

b) _____

_____

_____

_____

_____

Summary:

Look over your notes from this study. What attitudes can you cultivate that will enable you to be more like Peter and less like Judas?

1. How I can be more like Peter: _____

_____

_____

_____

2. How I can be less like Judas: _____

_____

_____

_____

Tip for Repentance:

Despair is a terrible thing. The example of Judas shows us that it can be something that actually cuts us off from God. If we totally abandon faith in his will to forgive our sins and save us from final damnation, we are, in fact, sinning against God by refusing to believe in what he has revealed—that is, his merciful love made manifest in Jesus Christ.

Therefore, it is important to remember that simply being anxious about our sins or feeling guilty are not the same thing as despair. These feelings are meant to drive us to repent and to resolve anew to follow the Lord's call just as Peter did. When we are tempted to despair, we may feel that it is inevitable—that some kind of irresistible force of logic is driving us to the conclusion that God hates us and we are doomed. This is not true. We can make the decision not to despair, but rather to turn to God in repentance. God has promised to forgive our sins when we repent. It is good to recall this truth constantly, so that it will be easier to remember when we need it, at the time when God seems far away. Try to develop the habit of thinking about God's mercy. This will prevent temptations to despair and drive them away when they occur.

Optional Memory Verse:

> *Let us fall into the hands of the* LORD
> *and not into the hands of men,*
> *For equal to his majesty*
> *is the mercy that he shows.* (Sir 2:18)

For Group Discussion:

1. Why is Peter's sin of denial nearly as bad as Judas' sin of betrayal?

2. What is crucial about Peter's response to the enormity of his sin in contrast to Judas' response? What can we learn from Peter's response? Discuss.

3. The risen Christ appears to Peter and some of the disciples in the last chapter of John's Gospel. In this incident, what exactly does Jesus say and do to indicate that Peter has been forgiven?

4. Share the summaries from your study with each other. Ask yourselves, "How I can be more like Peter and less like Judas?"

5. How can you develop the habit of thinking about God's mercy to drive away the temptation to despair? Have someone read the "Tip for Repentance" aloud and then answer this question.

Study 5—Luke 23:39-43
Failing to Grasp the Unlimited Mercy of God

Now one of the criminals hanging there reviled Jesus, saying, "Are you not the Messiah? Save yourself and us." The other, however, rebuking him, said in reply, "Have you no fear of God, for you are subject to the same condemnation? And indeed, we have been condemned justly, for the sentence we received corresponds to our crimes, but this man has done nothing criminal." Then he said, "Jesus, remember me when you come into your kingdom." He replied to him, "Amen, I say to you, today you will be with me in Paradise." (Lk 23:39-43)

We call him Dismas, but we don't really know his name. We don't know precisely what crime he was executed for. But we do know one thing about him. He is in heaven with Jesus.

Scripture presents us with the story of the two thieves who were crucified with Jesus to inspire us to believe in God's mercy. Just as we can think sometimes that some enormous sin makes us ineligible for God's forgiveness, many people struggle with believing that God can redeem them from a life of repeated and regular sin. "It's too late for me," we think, "I've sinned too many times for God to forgive me. I've lived a life far from God so long it's impossible for me ever to come to him." This is another form of the "God can't forgive me" syndrome: "I'm just too bad for God."

Luke just calls them "criminals"; Mark refers to them as "robbers."

45

The latter word might mean "highwaymen" or "plunderers," or even "terrorists." Whatever they had done, it involved a life characterized by stealing with violence. Perhaps they had killed in the course of their activities. Whatever they were, as Dismas admitted, their crimes deserved the harshest punishment: death by torture. The other criminal (an old tradition calls him Gestas) could only think of getting out of his punishment—to go back to thieving, perhaps.

Dismas recognized the seriousness of his sins. He had no desire to return to that life. He trusted in God and turned toward Jesus in the midst of all the pain and suffering of crucifixion. When every breath could only be drawn with the greatest pain, he spoke first to his former companion in crime, then he turned to Jesus. He turned to Jesus and he trusted. In response, he heard the beautiful, inspiring words: "Today you will be with me in Paradise." God's mercy is big enough to give paradise to one who in the last minute before death repents and turns to him. We should remember these words whenever we are tempted to say that we are too bad to be forgiven.

Another example we can remember is Paul—Paul, the great apostle to the Gentiles, author of numerous New Testament letters, and a great sinner. In the first letter to Timothy there is a much-quoted passage: "Christ Jesus came into the world to save sinners. Of these I am the foremost" (1 Tm 1:15). This is not merely a pious sentiment. While there may be some place for my saying, "I am the foremost of sinners"— certainly I know more of the evil of my own sin than of those of others—Paul had something else in mind here, something specific to himself. Paul tells Timothy what it was: "I was once a blasphemer and a persecutor and an arrogant man" (1 Tm 1:13). He is referring to his persecution of the church. We see clearly in Acts 8:1-3 that he participated in putting people to death for their faith in Christ. When Jesus appeared to Paul on the road to Damascus, he equated persecution of Christians with persecution of himself: "I am Jesus, whom you are persecuting" (Acts 9:5), words Paul recalled again and again. Paul had been guilty of persecuting Christ himself. Paul was the greatest of sinners because he had committed the greatest of sins.

While Paul always remembered his sinful past, he did not despair of God's mercy. Rather he pointed to his own redemption as evidence of God's grace. "For I am the least of the apostles, not fit to be called an apostle, because I persecuted the church of God. But by the grace of God I am what I am, and his grace to me has not been ineffective" (1 Cor 15:9-10). When Paul saw his sin, he repented and did not allow despair to interfere either with God's mercy or with the work God had called him to do.

Dismas and Paul, like Mary Magdalene and Peter, teach us that God's mercy can extend to any sin. We need never think that we cannot be forgiven. His grace is sufficient if only we repent and turn to him. Meditating on these words: "Today you will be with me in Paradise," addressed to the criminal who hung next to Jesus at his crucifixion, should bring us joy in being forgiven sinners. Like Paul, we can say, "By the grace of God I am what I am, and his grace to me has not been ineffective."

Study: Luke 23:39-43.

1. Read 2 Chronicles 33:1-20. Here we have the story of the repentance of King Manasseh. What kinds of sins did Manasseh commit?

_____

_____

What brought him to repentance?

_____

_____

How did he change his mind?

_____

_____

How did he manifest the fruits of repentance? Remember to number your points.

_____

_____

_____

_____

_____

2. The Book of Jonah is an inspired story about the unlimited mercy of God. Fill out the chart provided on the Book of Jonah. Scan the Scripture texts indicated to locate your answers.

The Scripture Passage and the Human Party Involved	The Situation	How the Human Party Responds	How God Shows Mercy
Jonah: the reluctant Prophet (Jon 1-2)			
The crew on the ship bound for Tarshish (Jon 1:4-16)			
The people of Nineveh (Jon 3)			
Jonah: angry with God after he has mercy on Nineveh (Jon 4)			

How is repentance a key to unlocking God's mercy in the Book of Jonah? Notice in particular Jonah's prayer in the belly of the fish (Jon 2:3-10) and the people of Nineveh's response to Jonah's preaching (Jon 3:5-10).

_____

_____

_____

_____

_____

What is the point of the Book of Jonah? What does it tell us about God's basic disposition toward human beings? See in particular Jonah 4:5-11.

a) _____

_____

_____

b) _____

_____

_____

3. Read Acts 9:1-30. This chapter describes the conversion of Saul (that is, Paul). What sin does Paul commit before his conversion?

_____

_____

What brings him to repentance?

_____

_____

How does he change his mind in repentance?

_____

_____

What does he do to manifest the fruits of repentance?

_____

_____

_____

_____

_____

4. Read Luke 23:39-43. This is all we know about the salvation of the thief on the cross. Both criminals allude to Jesus as the Messiah. How do they differ in their attitude toward him?

_____

_____

_____

_____

_____

How does the good thief ("Dismas") show repentance?

_____

_____

How does he manifest faith?

_____

_____

Compare Jesus' treatment of Dismas with his treatment of Mary Magdalene (Lk 7:36-50) and of Zacchaeus (Lk 19:1-10). What common points are there to the way Jesus deals with sinners?

(a) Comparison with Mary Magdalene: _____

_____

_____

_____

(b) Comparison with Zacchaeus: _____

_____

_____

_____

_____

Summary:

Look over your notes from this study. How can you apply the examples given by Manasseh, Jonah, Paul, and Dismas to your own life?

1. Manasseh: _____

_____

2. Jonah: _____

_____

3. Paul: _____

_____

4. Dismas: _____

_____

Tip for Repentance:

It's true that it's never too late to repent—as long as you're alive. The examples in this lesson show that God can take any life and turn it around, but that's still not a good reason to put off repenting. I had an experience some years ago that pointed this out clearly for me.

I was flying home from a conference with a fellow college dean in his small private plane when a surprise hailstorm came up, and we were caught in it. The plane twisted and bucked, and I was sure that my last moment had come. I turned to God, admitting that I'd done things I shouldn't have done and hadn't done things I should have. Then I offered him my whole life—which I thought would only last two minutes more—and told him I trusted in his mercy. At that moment I felt surrounded by the love of God. I felt nothing but peace and joy. I knew that Jesus had conquered death and that he was the resurrection and the life. I knew that I need have no fear of death or of things that bring about death, including sickness.

Since then I have seen my life change. I have been set free from the terrible fear of death that holds so many people in bondage. The grace I experienced in that plane has become a constant part of my life.

If the fruit of complete repentance and faith is so good, why wait until you can see the danger of death? Why wait until the last moment? Not only may death come at any time to any of us, but God's love and grace are too good a thing to waste. It's never too late to repent—but it's never too soon either.

Optional Memory Verse:

> *By the grace of God I am what I am, and his grace to me has not been ineffective.* (1 Cor 15:10)

For Group Discussion:

1. Why can the forgiving of Dismas be a great source of encouragement to us, especially in praying for family members and friends who need to be reconciled to God?

2. How is the apostle Paul's life another inspiring example of God's forgiveness and mercy for serious sin?

3. How does God demonstrate his great mercy to Jonah and the people of Nineveh? What is the relationship between repentance and the release of God's mercy when Jonah is delivered from the belly of the fish and the people of Nineveh are delivered from destruction? Discuss.

4. Consider for a moment how God has shown great mercy to you. Let everyone share a personal example of God's mercy.

5. Think of all of the repentant sinners in Scripture whose lives we have studied thus far. Whose example of repentance can you most identify with? Why? Discuss.

Study 6—Matthew 5:21-48
The Twilight Zone

If your right eye causes you to sin, tear it out and throw it away. It is better for you to lose one of your members than to have your whole body thrown into Gehenna. And if your right hand causes you to sin, cut it off and throw it away. It is better for you to lose one of your members than to have your whole body go into Gehenna. (Mt 5:29-30)

We usually don't think of it this way, but Jesus could be pretty harsh sometimes. In fact, the Gospels present him as being as merciless toward sin as he was merciful toward sinners. In the fifth chapter of Matthew's Gospel he takes the Old Testament law a step farther, making it more complete and demanding. In the process he shows us how to overcome an important barrier to the full effect of repentance in our lives.

Jesus explains in Matthew 5:17 that he has come "not to abolish but to fulfill" the law. He then proceeds to extend the scope of the law in accordance with a new principle. Now not only is murder forbidden, anyone who insults or bears anger against his brother is liable to judgment (Mt 5:21-22). Not only is adultery a crime, looking lustfully at a woman is equivalent to committing adultery with her (Mt 5:27-28). Then he says that we should be prepared to part with an eye or a hand if it leads us to sin. The things that lead to overt acts are also things we need to get out of our lives.

One reason why committed Christians still need to repent regularly is because they live their lives, or part of their lives, in what I have sometimes called the "twilight zone"—not exactly as children of darkness, but not as children of the light either.

Twilight can be a lovely time of day, but it doesn't last long. You know that pretty soon it's going to get dark. And living in the twilight inevitably leads to living in darkness. If we walk along the edge between good and evil for too long, we're bound to fall off. And even if the world, the flesh, and the devil are not pulling us toward sin, we still stand an even chance of sinning whenever we run such a risk. As it is, if we are inching away from God, the momentum is bound to carry us over the edge eventually.

The Lord showed me how this pattern of living in the twilight had been part of my life since my youth. It's probably true for a lot of people. How late could I stay out and still get home by the time my mother had told me? How far could I indulge in petting without sinning? How much could I borrow from reference books without being dishonest on papers? How much could I manipulate figures without actually cheating on my income tax? There were other areas in my "twilight zone," and there probably are in yours, too. I saw that my living in this way was focusing my life not on the Lord, but on the borderline between sin and virtue. In addition to running the risk of stepping over the edge into sin, I was behaving as if living for God were not a gift but a burden.

I needed to repent for the twilight areas, for exposing myself unnecessarily to sources of temptation. These are the things that traditional Catholic teaching calls "occasions of sin." They were indeed occasions of sin for me, for they inevitably led me into the sin I was trying to avoid. They are the kind of things Jesus was talking about when he told us, "If your right hand causes you to sin, cut it off and throw it away."

I don't know anybody whose right hand is the problem. It might be places you go that expose you to some temptation—stop going there. It might be a relationship that leads to sin—break it off. It might be a business that leads you to cheat—get out of it. It might be TV or movies that encourage lust, blasphemy, or denial of Christian truth—stop watching them.

This may seem harsh, but it's what Jesus says. After all, if we really want to avoid sin and live for the Lord, then no price can be too high to pay. As Paul says,

> Live as children of light, for light produces every kind of goodness and righteousness and truth. Try to learn what is pleasing to the Lord. Take no part in the fruitless works of darkness; rather expose them. (Eph 5:8-11)

Study: Matthew 5:21-48.

1. Read verses 21-26.
In this whole section of the Sermon on the Mount, Jesus is taking us through the "twilight zone." He is showing his hearers how many things that did not seem to violate the letter of the Old Testament law in fact violated its spirit. The commands of Jesus here can help us to see what twilight areas of our own lives are leading us into sin.

In verses 21-22, Jesus equates the use of abusive language with murder, since hatred leads to murder. Does insulting language have any part in my relationships? Try to be as specific as possible and list your points.

_____

_____

_____

Verses 23-26 speak of reconciliation. How can I be reconciled with people who may have something against me?

_____

_____

_____

_____

_____

2. Read verses 27-32.
In these verses Jesus holds up a high standard of purity and fidelity in marriage and sexual relationships. How have I lived up to this standard? Do I allow sexual desires to occupy my thoughts so they become occasions for sin?

a) _____

_____

b) _____

_____

The area of sexual desire and sexual relationships is a particularly hard one to handle in modern society. We need to be on guard to protect ourselves from dangerous situations and occasions of sin. What steps can I take to safeguard myself in this area?

_____

_____

_____

_____

_____

In Matthew 19:1-12, Jesus develops his teaching on marriage. What reason does he give for declaring marriage indissoluble?

_____

_____

_____

What alternative does Jesus offer to his teaching on marriage?

_____

_____

How have I lived up to Jesus' teaching in my own state in life, whether single or married?

_____

_____

_____

3. Read verses 33-48.
In these verses Jesus talks about honesty and generosity. Notice that keeping our promises and doing good, even to our enemies, are not

options but commands. How have I lived up to these teachings in my own life?

(a) Keeping promises: _____

_____

_____

(b) Doing good: _____

_____

_____

In verses 39-42, Jesus commands us to be willing not to retaliate, but rather to freely offer whatever we can. How have I put this teaching into effect?

_____

_____

_____

_____

_____

In Matthew 18:21-22 and Luke 17:3-4, Jesus gives us strong commands to forgive all who wrong us. Is there anyone in my life I have not forgiven? Have I sought forgiveness of all those I have wronged?

_____

_____

_____

_____

In verses 43-48, Jesus gives the Father as a standard of perfect love. What is it about God the Father that demonstrates this love?

Jesus commands us to be perfect in the same way. What can I do to put this command into effect? How is this possible?

a) _____

_____

b) _____

_____

Summary:

Look over your notes from this study. What have you learned about occasions of sin in your own life? What do you plan to do about it?

1. What I've learned: _____

2. What I plan to do about it: _____

_____

_____

_____

_____

Tip for Repentance:

One notable characteristic of twilight is that it is dim. The same applies to the twilight zone in our lives. We can't see things very clearly. When we ask ourselves about it, we are apt to make excuses or to say, "Well, I'm not *actually* sinning." We might instead ask questions like the following:

When have I asked myself, "How far can I go without sinning"? (You've probably gone too far.)

When have I called something a "white lie?" (The only definite thing we know about a white lie is that it's a lie.)

When have I said, "Charity begins at home," or "Look out for Number One first?" (You've probably sinned through selfishness.)

When did I say about my actions, "It's not that bad?" (You've already admitted that it's somewhat bad.)

When have I participated in a conversation that involved such phrases as, "I don't want to say anything against her, but . . . ?" (What followed "but" probably damaged her reputation.)

When have I said, "I really shouldn't be telling you this, but . . . ?" (Well, if you shouldn't, don't. You're probably betraying a confidence.)

Probing these areas may uncover areas of twilight you weren't aware of, areas where the Lord wants you to be free.

Optional Memory Verse:

"So be perfect, just as your heavenly Father is perfect." (Mt 5:48)

For Group Discussion:

1. Give an example of how Jesus takes the Old Testament law a step farther in the Sermon on the Mount. Along with your example, explain Jesus' reason for taking the law a step farther in that particular instance. Give everyone in the group a chance to share an example and then explain it to the group.

2. What exactly is the "twilight zone" in our Christian lives? Discuss.

3. What do you think Jesus would have us do when we flirt with "occasions of sin?" Why?

4. In the Sermon on the Mount, what does Jesus say about keeping promises and doing good? Why does Jesus consider honesty and generosity so important? Discuss.

5. Have someone read the "Tip for Repentance" aloud. Discuss the areas of twilight that are mentioned. Can you think of other areas as well?

Part III

A Life of Ongoing Conversion

It isn't enough simply to avoid occasions of sin. God expects more of us and wants to do far more for us. He calls us to a life of ongoing conversion and repentance. Repentance isn't just a once-in-a-lifetime event; we need to turn to God in repentance for sin throughout our lives. And the good news is God doesn't expect us to do it on our own, which would lead us to failure and despair. Rather, he offers us grace to overcome patterns of sin in our lives, particularly through the sacrament of reconciliation or penance. As we repent and God forgives our sins, he also desires to release healing into our lives. He frequently uses both the sacrament of the anointing of the sick and the sacrament of reconciliation to minister healing to us. During our last three studies, then, we will learn the importance of living a life of ongoing conversion to Christ and repentance of our sins.

Study 7—Romans 12:1-21
Ongoing Conversion

I urge you therefore, brothers, by the mercies of God, to offer your bodies as a living sacrifice, holy and pleasing to God, your spiritual worship. Do not conform yourself to this age but be transformed by the renewal of your mind, that you may discern what is the will of God, what is good and pleasing and perfect. (Rom 12:1-2)

Turning to God in repentance, especially when we haven't done it before or haven't done it in a long time, can be a wonderful experience. All of a sudden we experience God in a new way. But we need to be honest. This one experience will not provide us with all the holiness we need, so that we will never sin again. It's like some of the "Liberty Ships" that were built so quickly during the early days of World War II to speed us on to victory. There would be a great big launching with flags waving. Everything would appear to be fine. But then the great ship would slide down the slipway and sink.

When we find that we still sin, even after we have turned to the Lord, we can have several reactions. We can give up, deciding it's just too hard. We can develop a kind of spiritual schizophrenia, pretending on the outside that everything's all right, while we're screaming inside. Or we can try to make it on our own by will power, missing the power of the cross. All of these approaches ignore a basic principle of the Christian life, one that Paul refers to in Romans 12—that God's transforming power is always at work in us to bring about ongoing conversion.

God wants more of you than you want. God has more power available than you expect. As Paul says, "Offer your bodies as a living sacrifice." Old Testament worship involved offering the bodies of animals. The "spiritual worship" of the New Covenant involves the offering of our whole selves, here represented by imagining ourselves as animals being sacrificed on the altar.

This sacrifice takes place, as Paul goes on to explain, within the body of Christ—the church—where each member has some gift to contribute. The regulations of this new worship are not the physical and ritual rules of the Old Testament, but the rule of love expressed in verse 10 of Romans 12. Offering ourselves completely to God makes it possible for his power to transform and renew our minds, so that we conform to his standards and not to those of the present world around us.

Paul experienced this himself. His description of himself in Romans 7:21-25 could apply to many of us. We find when we try to do right that we somehow end up doing wrong. All of creation, he says in Romans 8:22, is groaning as in labor with the process of ongoing conversion—and so are we.

We find ongoing conversion by looking at God's law, God's Word, God's ways, and repenting constantly when we see ourselves straying from them. Realizing that ongoing conversion is part of the Christian life and that it is God's work can free us from much useless striving. It can make the struggles we face occasions of joy, rather than depression.

One area in which I have experienced ongoing conversion is in my speech. I had developed the habit of speaking of the Franciscan men with whom I lived in a way that damaged their reputations. I did not tell lies about them, but I spoke of them in a way that emphasized their failings. I would speak of one brother's temper, another's intolerance, and other bad habits that I noticed. If the brother was present, I might kid him about it. If he was absent, I might tell stories that caused others to laugh at him.

For a long time, although I had a vague sense that this was wrong, I continued to follow this bad pattern. Then one day after I had heard a teaching on speech, I took some time to pray. As I prayed, I saw how deeply I had sinned in my speech. I was moved to repentance and great grief over how I had offended my brothers.

I asked God for forgiveness, and I went to my confessor in the sacrament of reconciliation. I resolved to pray for the brothers I had offended and to engage only in speech that was uplifting and built up my brothers' reputations. Since then I have experienced not only a change in the way I speak, but also much greater peace in my conversations. They are a source of well-being for me in a way they never were before.

When we come to Jesus in repentance, again and again, he makes us, little by little, into what he wants us to be. We can never overcome our weakness and sin by ourselves, but as Paul writes in Romans 8:37: "In all these things we conquer overwhelmingly through him who loved us."

Study: Romans 12:1-21.

1. Read verses 1-3.
Here Paul talks about the way in which we are supposed to approach ongoing conversion. What is our part in this conversion supposed to be?

_____

_____

What is God's part?

_____

_____

_____

Paul exhorts us not to be conformed "to this age," that is, to the present world and to the society around us. How do I need to oppose the tendencies inherent in this present age? List some of the main tendencies of this sort that you've noticed.

a) _____

_____

_____

b) _____

_____

_____

In verse 3, Paul speaks of how we are to view ourselves. He also brings up this theme in Philippians 2:1-11. What is the attitude we are to have toward ourselves? When we have this kind of attitude, who are we imitating? How?

a) _____

_____

_____

b) _____

_____

2. Read verses 4-8.

An important aspect of conversion is using the gifts God has given us for the good of the whole church. What kind of gifts does Paul talk about here? How are they to be used?

a) _____

_____

_____

b) _____

_____

_____

Compare what Paul says here with what Peter says in 1 Peter 4:10-11. How do we have the ability to serve? What is the purpose of our service?

a) _____

_____

_____

b) _____

_____

_____

Compare these passages with Ephesians 4:11-16. How does the work of the church contribute to ongoing conversion? Be specific.

_____

_____

_____

_____

_____

How am I putting this teaching into effect in my own life? Mention two areas.

a) _____

_____

_____

b) _____

_____

3. Read verses 9-21.
Consider for a moment the way of life described here. What attitudes are required to live in this way? List them below.

_____

_____

_____

_____

_____

Compare this passage with the description in Colossians 3:5-17 of the old life and the new life. What are the qualities that are to be "put to death"? Don't forget to number your points.

_____

_____

_____

_____

_____

What are those that are to be "put on?"

_____

_____

_____

_____

_____

What can a person do to "put on" the kind of qualities that God desires?

_____

_____

_____

_____

_____

How am I putting this teaching into effect in my own life? Try to think of at least one important way you're putting this into practice.

_____

_____

_____

_____

_____

Summary:

Look over your notes from this study. How has the Lord led you into ongoing conversion? How is he calling you to ongoing conversion today?

1. Ongoing conversion in the past: _____

_____

_____

_____

_____

2. Ongoing conversion in the present: _____

_____

_____

_____

_____

Tip for Repentance:

Ongoing conversion is not a matter of adopting stricter rules of life or ascetic practices. It is not something we accomplish on our own efforts or by mere willpower. It cannot be accomplished except through the cross of Jesus Christ. We need to bear this truth in mind when we seek to live up to the standards set for us in the Scriptures.

What is really essential to ongoing conversion is faith. We need to believe that God loves us and wants to have a close relationship with us, a relationship that can only come as we are transformed into his likeness. We need to believe in his Word and trust that we can depend on it. The life that God wants us to have with him is his idea; we only need to trust him. It takes genuine trust to renounce underhanded practices when they seem like the easiest way to get what we want. It takes trust to refuse to take revenge or to "get ours back." But when God commands something, he gives the grace to accomplish it. In order to be able to live the way God wants us to, the first thing to pray for is faith, instead of trying to muster up willpower on our own.

Optional Memory Verse:

Do not conform yourself to this age but be transformed by the renewal of your mind, that you may discern what is the will of God, what is good and pleasing and perfect. (Rom 12:2)

For Group Discussion:

1. Why do you think repentance and conversion are not just once-in-a-lifetime events but part of an ongoing process? Discuss.

2. How does Paul say that we can experience this ongoing conversion in our lives? Specifically, what is it that we need to do?

3. What are some of the common tendencies in American society that war against our ongoing conversion to Christ? Discuss.

4. How can using the gifts that God has given help to convert us to his ways?

5. Why is faith essential for ongoing conversion and repentance from sin? Discuss.

Study 8—John 20:19-23
The Sacrament of Penance

On the evening of that first day of the week, when the doors were locked, where the disciples were, for fear of the Jews, Jesus came and stood in their midst and said to them, "Peace be with you." When he had said this, he showed them his hands and his side. The disciples rejoiced when they saw the Lord. Jesus said to them again, "Peace be with you. As the Father has sent me, so I send you." And when he had said this, he breathed on them and said to them, "Receive the holy Spirit. Whose sins you forgive are forgiven them, and whose sins you retain are retained." (Jn 20:19-23)

Only God can forgive sins. That's what the scribes thought when they heard Jesus declare that the paralyzed man's sins were forgiven (Mk 2:6-7). They were right, but as the only-begotten Son of God, Jesus had a unique authority to forgive sins. Yet here in this appearance to his disciples after the resurrection, Jesus declares that he is giving them the same power that he himself has: to forgive sins, a prerogative of God himself.

It is this power given to the apostles, with a special gift of the Holy Spirit, that is the basis for the sacrament of penance. It is mentioned right here in the Scriptures. By this sacrament the church continues the ministry of Jesus. As Paul wrote to the Corinthians concerning his work as an apostle, "God was reconciling the world to himself in Christ, not counting their trespasses against them and entrusting to us the message of reconciliation" (2 Cor 5:19). The church carries out the ministry of reconciliation by means of this sacrament, which is the sacrament of reconciliation. This sacrament is God's gift to us. It enables us to repent from the heart and to stay free of serious sin thereafter.

In spite of the great value of this gift, however, the sacrament of penance has been a troubling one for the church in recent years. Many people rarely receive the sacrament. Others feel that little happens in it. Changes in the way the sacrament is celebrated have confused some people and caused them to struggle and to feel guilty about its place, or lack of place, in their lives.

Part of the problem lies in a failure to appreciate the seriousness of sin and the need for repentance. Another part of the problem is having a correct understanding of the place of the sacrament of penance in the Lord's plan for our lives.

Whenever we repent from the heart, even privately, God does forgive us. True, complete, heartfelt repentance is what traditional Catholic teaching calls "perfect contrition." But often we fail to have perfect contrition because we do not completely grasp the seriousness of our sin. Or we do not have sufficient determination to change. The sacrament of penance provides the grace necessary to transform our inadequate attempts to repent into a perfect turning to the Lord. Even if we do not avail ourselves of it, the grace is there. Also, part of perfect contrition is the desire to confess our sins and receive the grace of God available in the sacrament, accepting the ministry of reconciliation that the Lord has given to his church. Thus we always need the sacrament of penance. The more often we receive it, the more the Lord will be able to work in our lives.

While a holy and gifted priest makes the best confessor, the grace of the sacrament of penance does not depend on the priest's character or ability, but on the promise of Jesus Christ to his church. You should never let dislike of a particular priest deter you from turning to the Lord and receiving the blessings of reconciliation. You should concentrate on God's grace and your contrition.

There are four steps that we can take in order to profit most from the grace of this sacrament. First, we should pray for the Holy Spirit to reveal to us what in our own behavior is sinful. Second, we need to understand what is the righteous way to live in Christ. We need to know God's Word and the teaching of the church, as well as going to the Lord and asking for his guidance. Third, we should pray for the strength to turn from sin to the ways of God. We can't do it on our own, but God will give us the grace if we ask him. Finally, we need to seek guidance and help to maintain our resolve to live for the Lord. Ideally, if we need prayers of healing, the priest will pray for us before the confession is completed.

There is real power in this sacrament to change our lives. Jesus came to preach repentance and conversion, and he has left the Holy Spirit to his church to continue this ministry. When we make use of the sacrament of penance, we are coming to Jesus as Mary Magdalene did. We are hearing his word of forgiveness in a tangible way, a word that empowers us to love and serve God and others.

Study: John 20:19-23.

1. Read John 20:19-23.
How are the disciples going to participate in the mission of Jesus?

Evangelization + forgiving sinners

What will give them the power to do what Jesus commands?

The Holy Spirit

Compare this passage with Matthew 16:13-20. What sort of authority is Peter being given here?

The authority to become a Church + teach his divine truths.

Compare this passage with Matthew 18:15-20. What do these words of Jesus tell us about his work through the church?

By following Church teaching we can determine what is just + moral in our actions toward others.

2. In several places in the New Testament, we see the apostles, especially Peter and Paul, using their apostolic authority in different ways. For each of the Scripture passages listed in the chart I have provided, note the following: How is this authority being used? What is its purpose? How does God work through it? Observe especially how the apostles

either call sinners to repent or exercise a ministry of reconciliation in these passages, depending upon the particular situation. Answer these questions by scanning the Scriptures and then by filling out the chart.

The Scripture Passage	How Is This Apostolic Authority Used?	What Is Its Purpose?	How Does God Work Through It?
Acts 2:14-39 esp. v. 38			
Acts 3:1-26 esp. vv. 19-23			
Acts 11:1-18 esp. v. 18			
1 Corinthians 5:1-5			
2 Corinthians 2:5-11			
2 Corinthians 7:5-13			

Why do you think Christ gave this kind of authority to the apostles?

_____

_____

_____

_____

3. Read 2 Corinthians 5:16-21.
Here Paul presents the ministry of reconciliation. In it, God the Father, Christ, and the church each has a part. What is the part played by God the Father?

_____

_____

_____

What is the part Christ has to play?

_____

_____

_____

What is the church's part in the ministry of reconciliation?

_____

_____

_____

How are each of us, as members of the church, called to share in this ministry of reconciliation?

_____

_____

Paul points out that this ministry of reconciliation enables us to be "ambassadors for Christ." And he implores us "on behalf of Christ, be reconciled to God." What does this tell us about the connection between repenting of sin in our own lives and being an effective witness for Christ?

_____

_____

_____

_____

_____

_____

How does this teaching apply to your life? Can you think of at least two specific applications at home or at work?

_____

_____

_____

_____

_____

What does this tell us about the way sin affects our relationships with others?

_____

_____

_____

_____

Summary:

Look over your notes from this study. How have you come to a better scriptural understanding of the sacrament of penance? How will this affect the way you approach the sacrament in the future?

1. My scriptural understanding: _____

_____

_____

_____

2. My approach to the sacrament: _____

_____

_____

_____

_____

_____

Tip for Repentance:

Throughout its history, the church has especially valued Psalm 51 as a prayer of repentance. This psalm, according to its title in the Book of Psalms, was written by David after the prophet Nathan called him to repent for his adultery with Bathsheba. Its words embody a clear teaching on repentance.

David begins by confessing and asking for mercy. He recognizes the seriousness of his sin against God and his utter need for forgiveness. He then asks God not only to forgive his serious sin but to renew him, to give him "a clean heart." He recognizes that complete conversion can only come from God. He concludes by offering praise to God and promising to serve God faithfully in the future. All the parts of repentance are here. This psalm, inspired by the Holy Spirit, is the perfect prayer of repentance.

Praying Psalm 51 is a good way to prepare to receive the sacrament of penance. If you can make David's prayer your own, you will have the right disposition to receive not only God's forgiveness but his power for freedom and conversion.

Optional Memory Verse:

> *God was reconciling the world to himself in Christ, not counting their trespasses against them and entrusting to us the message of reconciliation.* (2 Cor 5:19)

For Group Discussion:

1. What is the scriptural basis for the sacrament of penance or reconciliation? Discuss.

2. What kind of authority did Jesus give the apostles in the New Testament? How do we see the apostles exercise it in the Book of Acts and the Pauline Epistles?

3. How does the sacrament of penance or reconciliation help us live a life of ongoing repentance and conversion? What does the Lord do for us in this sacrament when we approach it with the right attitude of heart?

4. Discuss the four steps that can help us profit the most from the sacrament of penance.

5. Have someone read the "Tip for Repentance," and then have someone else read Psalm 51. Reflect together on how this psalm provides a model prayer for repentance. Consider using the psalm to prepare for confession.

Study 9—Mark 2:1-12
Repentance and Healing

When Jesus saw their faith, he said to the paralytic, "Child, your sins are forgiven." Now some of the scribes were sitting there asking themselves, "Why does this man speak that way? He is blaspheming. Who but God alone can forgive sins?" Jesus immediately knew in his mind what they were thinking to themselves, so he said, "Why are you thinking such things in your hearts? Which is easier, to say to the paralytic, 'Your sins are forgiven,' or to say, 'Rise, pick up your mat and walk?' But that you may know that the Son of Man has authority to forgive sins on earth"— he said to the paralytic, "I say to you, rise, pick up your mat, and go home." He rose, picked up his mat at once, and went away in the sight of everyone. They were all astounded and glorified God, saying, "We have never seen anything like this." (Mk 2:5-12)

Jesus seems to have had an easy time healing people. Mark's Gospel begins with a series of healings which are presented as effortless, natural incidents in Jesus' ministry: a demon-possessed man, a leper, and Peter's mother-in-law. We might not think that healing is easy, but Jesus certainly did it without much effort.

People saw it, too. When Jesus went somewhere, they flocked to see him, and they brought those who needed to be healed. The need was obvious, and Jesus healed them. This story from Mark 2 demonstrates that Jesus' ministry had attracted many people's attention. When one enterprising group couldn't get their paralyzed friend in through the door, they lowered him through the roof. Then Jesus added something new to what everyone was expecting. Instead of telling the man to be healed, he told him that his sins were forgiven.

The onlookers were shocked. Jesus asked them, "Which is easier, to tell him his sins are forgiven, or to tell him to walk?" Then he healed the man, pointing out that this was a sign that he could also forgive sins.

Notice that the crowd didn't have any difficulty believing that Jesus could heal. That's opposite to the reaction that we might have today. We think, "Forgiveness is just a matter of words, but healing is something real and tangible." But forgiveness of sins is really the hard part. Sin is an offense against the nature of the holy God. It took the death of Jesus on the cross to give us the access to forgiveness that we have as Christians. For God, healing is the easy part.

In the story of the man born blind in John's Gospel, Jesus makes it clear that infirmity is not always the result of personal sin (Jn 9:2-3). Yet in this story from Mark, healing and forgiveness do go together. Forgiveness comes first, because to be reconciled to God is of eternal importance, while sickness or infirmity is something that only applies in this passing world. But God loves us and also wants to give us the blessings of healing, just as Jesus did for so many during his ministry on earth.

The church continues this ministry both of healing and of reconciliation, as James demonstrates by linking the two in his letter:

> Is anyone among you sick? He should summon the presbyters of the church, and they should pray over him and anoint him with oil in the name of the Lord, and the prayer of faith will save the sick person, and the Lord will raise him up. If he has committed any sins, he will be forgiven. Therefore confess your sins to one another and pray for one another, that you may be healed. (Jas 5:14-16)

This passage is the basis for the sacrament of the anointing of the sick which—while it is often a sacrament of healing—has as its principal effect the forgiveness of sins.

In addition, I have seen in my own ministry and in that of other priests, many healings of physical symptoms and of psychological and emotional difficulties come through the sacrament of reconciliation. When we are reconciled to God through repentance, his power is more able to work in us for healing.

If you truly believe that God can forgive your sins, then you should also believe that he can heal you. It only makes sense. The two really do go together in Jesus' ministry and that of the apostles. As Paul writes, "He who did not spare his own Son but handed him over for us all, how will he not give us everything else along with him?" (Rom 8:32)

Study: Mark 2:1-12.

1. Read Mark 2:1-12.
This account in Scripture tells us something about healing and something about who Jesus is. It also presents a pattern of the way the Lord often works in our lives. First we see the paralytic's friends going to great length to bring him to Jesus.

When they finally get into the house, to what does Jesus respond?

_____

_____

How has this been demonstrated?

_____

_____

What can we infer from this story about who Jesus is?

_____

_____

_____

How has Jesus manifested who he is in this story?

_____

_____

_____

_____

_____

How does this pattern apply to my own life?

_____

_____

_____

_____

_____

2. Read Isaiah 38:1-20.

This passage recounts the sickness and healing of Hezekiah, king of Judah. When Hezekiah discovers that he is mortally ill, what is his first reaction?

_____

_____

How does the Lord respond to him?

_____

_____

By what means does the Lord heal him?

_____

_____

After he is healed, Hezekiah prays to the Lord. What connection does he make between sin and sickness?

_____

_____

_____

_____

_____

Of all the kings of Israel and Judah, Hezekiah is one of the most highly praised as an example of a man who was faithful to the Lord (see Sir 49:4). What can we learn from Hezekiah about how to respond to sickness? What does this mean for me when I get sick?

a) _____

_____

_____

_____

_____

b) _____

_____

_____

_____

_____

3. Read James 5:13-20.
Sickness is not the only concern of James in this passage. In verse 13 he mentions two other circumstances. What general attitude toward the circumstances of our life is he encouraging?

_____

_____

_____

_____

_____

Compare this passage with Mark 6:7-13. How do the presbyters— the priests or elders—continue the mission of the twelve apostles?

_____

_____

_____

_____

_____

Look at the three questions and answers in verses 13-14. Then fill out the chart provided.

The Scripture Passage	The Question	The Answer	How It Shows the Power of Prayer
Question and Answer #1 (v. 13)			
Question and Answer #2 (v. 13)			
Question and Answer #3 (v. 14)			

Did you notice that in only one of the answers does James direct that someone else other than the person immediately affected be involved in the prayer? What exactly is James saying here by linking healing and forgiveness with the ministry of the presbyters or elders of the church?

_____

_____

_____

_____

_____

_____

Summary:

Look over your notes from this study. What principles can you observe about how God works in healing? How have these principles been active in your life?

1. Principles for healing: _____

_____

_____

_____

_____

2. How these principles have been active in my life: _____

_____

_____

_____

Tip for Repentance:

There are a lot of books written about healing, setting forth various theories and principles about how God works to heal people. I've written one myself, in fact. Reading them can be a helpful way of learning more about this important work of God, since they contain a lot more than can be said here.

One thing all these books stress is the role of faith in healing. Faith must always be present in order for God to heal. Sometimes the faith is that of the person being prayed with. Sometimes that person has no faith or very little, but the person praying for the healing has faith that God will heal in this particular case. Sometimes, as in Mark 2, the faith of someone else on behalf of the sick person enables the Lord to heal.

In any case, when we are praying for healing, we should pray for faith. Faith is not some kind of superior willpower. It is a supernatural gift from God. Some faith is necessary for any kind of prayer, or for receiving God's forgiveness, but often the Lord wants to give us a special gift of faith for healing, a faith infused with certainty and confidence. I have seen this gift operate in my own ministry, and dramatic healings follow as a result.

The most prudent thing to do is to pray for this faith, even before praying for healing.

Optional Memory Verse:

Therefore confess your sins to one another and pray for one another, that you may be healed. (Jas 5:16)

For Group Discussion:

1. In the Gospels, how does Jesus combine forgiveness of sins with a ministry of healing?

2. Why is the forgiveness of sins more important than the healing? Discuss.

3. What is the biblical basis for the sacrament of the anointing of the sick? What exactly does Christ do for us in this sacrament?

4. Can God also use the sacrament of reconciliation to bring healing into our lives? How?

5. How can the practice of repentance and ever-increasing faith in God open up our lives to his healing touch? Discuss.